INDIGO ANIMAL™

PORCH LION PRESS
PO Box 5008 Berkeley CA 94705

Indigo Animal and the Lawn Statuary Research Institute
Copyright © 2005 by Rue Harrison Whittaker
All rights reserved. No part of this publication may be reproduced
or transmitted in any form or by any means, electronic or mechanical, including
photocopy, recording, or any information storage and retrieval system,
without permission in writing from Porch Lion Press.

"Indigo Animal" has been registered by the United States Trademark and Patent Office.

Excerpts have been previously published in *works + conversations* Issue #6, 2002;
Issue #7, 2003; Issue #8, 2004; Issue #9, 2004, Issue #10, 2005.

To order by phone call *works + conversations* at: 510.653.1146
To order by fax: 510.594.8713
To order on line: http://www.IndigoAnimal.com
(or use the order form on the last page of this book)

ISBN: 0-9667279-1-6

Indigo Animal

and the Lawn Statuary Research Institute

written and illustrated by

Rue Harrison

PORCH LION PRESS

P.O. Box 5008 Berkeley CA 94705

For my Father
Donald Bilbrough Harrison
and
in memory of my Mother
Amelia Mahan Harrison

FROM THE AUTHOR

Indigo Animal and the Lawn Statuary Research Institute is the second book in an ongoing series. If you've read the first book, *Indigo Animal,* you needn't read further. You already know that Indigo is perhaps "overly serious." You understand that Indigo Animal, possessing circumspection and a refined sensibility, is out of step in a world in which such virtues seem to have been left behind. You also know that beneath Indigo's reserve and shyness, a hidden passion has been awakened which may lead this determined ungulate far from the path of predictability.

However, if you haven't yet read the first book, stop here, get your checkbook and purchase one immediately!* If, on the other hand, you are impatient and can't wait to read the book you *do* have, then I invite you to take part in a brief and relaxing exercise to help you get into the spirit of the story so far.

*there's an order form at the back of the book

Take a few deep breaths.

Now flip a few pages and study Indigo Animal, a four-footed creature, yet with very sensitive front feet, feet that might do rather well with a computer keyboard.

Imagine Indigo Animal hunkered down on a blanket in a bright, barren, Mediterranean landscape, possibly a remote part of the Peloponnesus. Here and there deep pits have been dug. Artifacts are lying all around this scene: statues, columns, amphorae, sarcophagi. A large striped bearcat, coated with dust, is digging feverishly in one of the pits while an odd, squinty-eyed old rodent examines and sorts pottery shards into different piles. In front of Indigo Animal is a laptop computer. Imagine this scene until you can hear the soft sound of the computer keys clicking as Indigo Animal types an e-mail to me, the author.

Dear Rue,

*Received your latest ms and have been poring over it with a mixture of pleasure and anxiety. I feel a little uncomfortable revisiting the **most** awkward phase in my progress as a lawn statuary researcher. I see you have taken some poetic license with the details.*

Can I be honest? The problem that I have with the book is this: how will a new reader know how unsentient my life had been before I turned the corner, as it were, and beheld that first birdbath? You know what I mean. There was a point in time when a new way of seeing began to occur and there were many little steps that led up to it, all of which are well-chronicled in your first book.

Readers beginning with Book Two will not know about all the time spent, all the years wasted lying around the house, hypnotized by the TV and munching goodies! (True, I watched only the nature channel, golf, and a few game shows.) What about the shock I experienced after that bunch of squirrels stole my television? What about the depression which followed that loss?

How can they understand <u>this</u> book if they do not know about that turning point when the theme song from Jeopardy *finally stopped playing in my head? There were so many things that opened up after that, leading to the pure bliss of studying lawn statuary with—I remember how it came to me as if it were yesterday— ' a mind like a lawn mower recently delivered home by a good repairman.'*

Of course you'll remember my increasing forays into the neighborhood beyond the known territory, and how it was on just such an adventure that I found the matchbook cover advertising the Lawn Statuary Research Institute! After that, it seemed that my dream of sharing a passion for Classical Lawn Statuary with like-minded animals actually might be within reach.

It is important for everyone to know how noticing just one little thing can change everything!

Once I found the Institute, really, there was no going back. I just keep trying to learn what I can every step of the way.

I'd better sign off now and get back to the dig. You'll be gratified to know that both Dame Eleanor and Orange Bearcat have spent hours with your ms, annotating their copies and cross-referencing. Don't ask me what they think of your portrayal of them. I'm staying out of it.

Indigo Animal

RH, April 2005

CHAPTER ONE
First Day On Campus

Unless one is looking very intently, one might never know that the Lawn Statuary Research Institute exists at all!

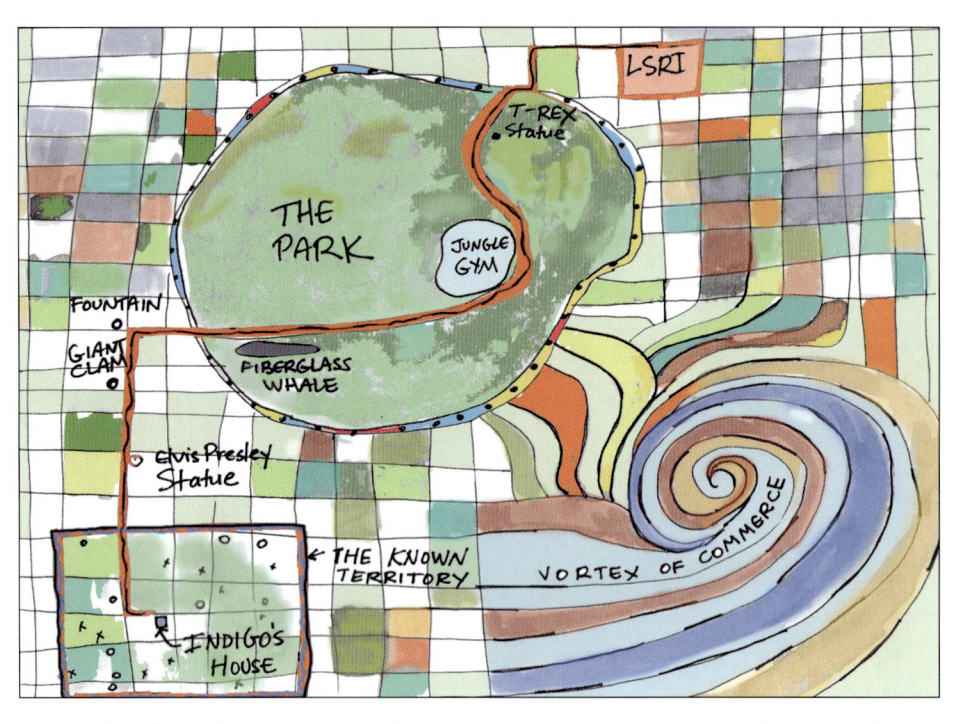

Having left the comfort of the known territory and entered the world, and after finding the entrance, Indigo Animal nudges the gate open.

Once inside, Indigo Animal finds an intricate maze of hedges.

Now and then, there's a tantalizing glimpse of what lies ahead.

But then, dismay!

Looking around, Indigo wonders, "Is it too late for a refund?"

Uneasy, Indigo continues to the center of campus—Orange Bearcat Hall—

and notices other students. They seem self-confident, relaxed, and smart.

Shyly joining a cluster of Freshmen, Indigo watches as a student shows the group her textbook for the class, *Modern Trends in Lawn Statuary*.

The other students seem very excited about it.

A bell rings and they all head off for the Modern Trends class. But Indigo's class meets in the Classical Studies building, which is nowhere to be seen.

"Pardon me, would you happen to know the way to the Classical Studies building?" Indigo asks a helpful squirrel running late to class.

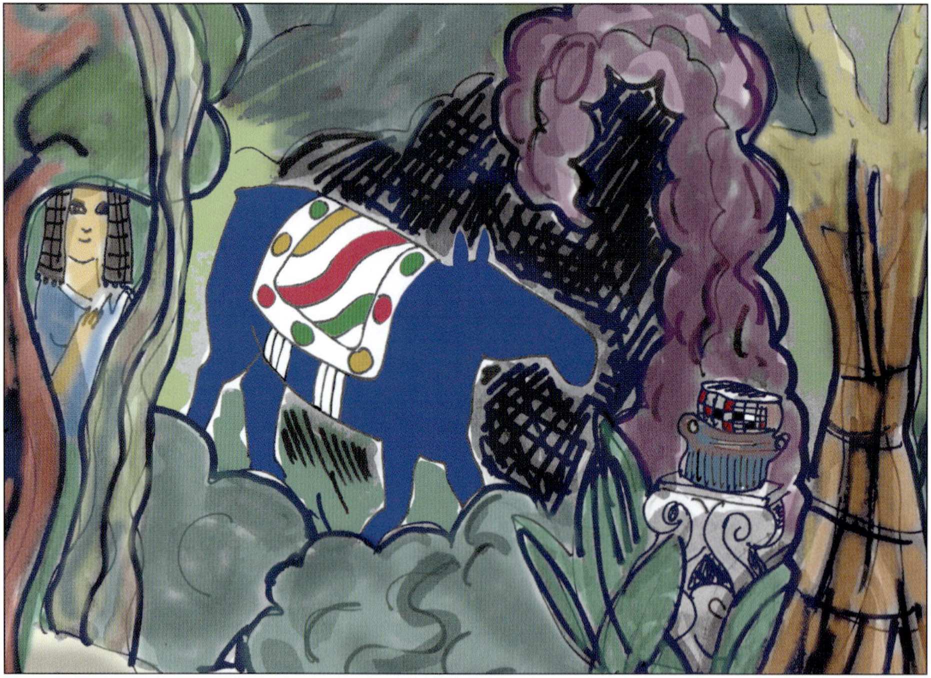

Walking along the secluded path, Indigo Animal, unsettled from the novelty of so much social contact, gradually feels centered again, and, beginning to enjoy the walk, notes that examples of classical forms have been cleverly placed in the bracken. Thus absorbed, Indigo is hardly prepared when the pathway suddenly opens up.

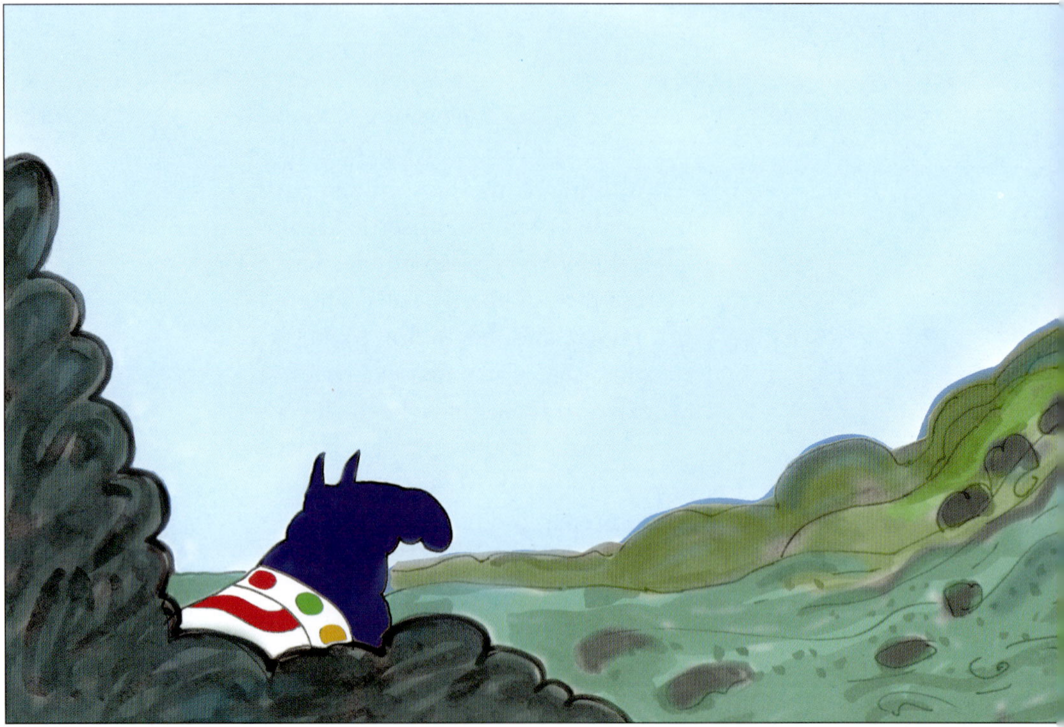

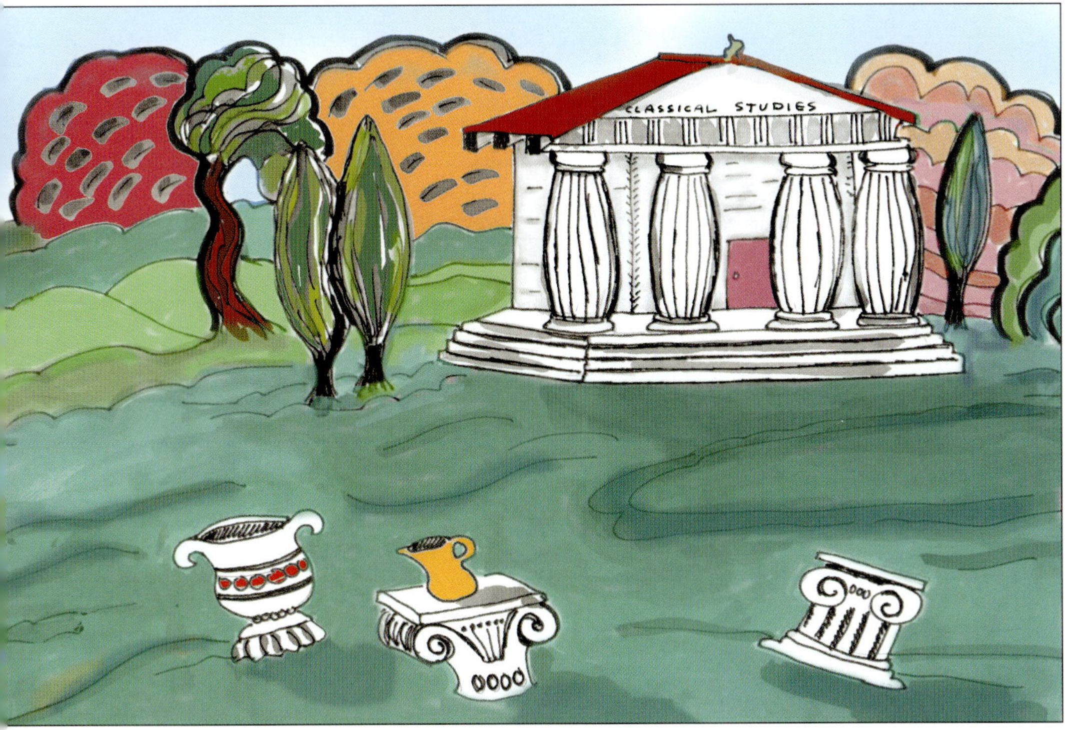
CLASSICAL STUDIES

CHAPTER TWO
The Classical Lawn Statuary Studies Department

"At last!" thinks Indigo Animal.

"Now my education can really begin."

The class is taught by Dame Eleanor Marmot, an ancient rodent.

Engrossed in the study of a pile of pottery shards on her desk, she seems not to notice Indigo Animal or the two other class members, foreign exchange students, Yeti and Wombat.

Wombat greets Indigo Animal.

Yeti shyly introduces herself.

Any more conversation is cut short as Dame Eleanor begins to mumble.

They all turn towards her with interest.

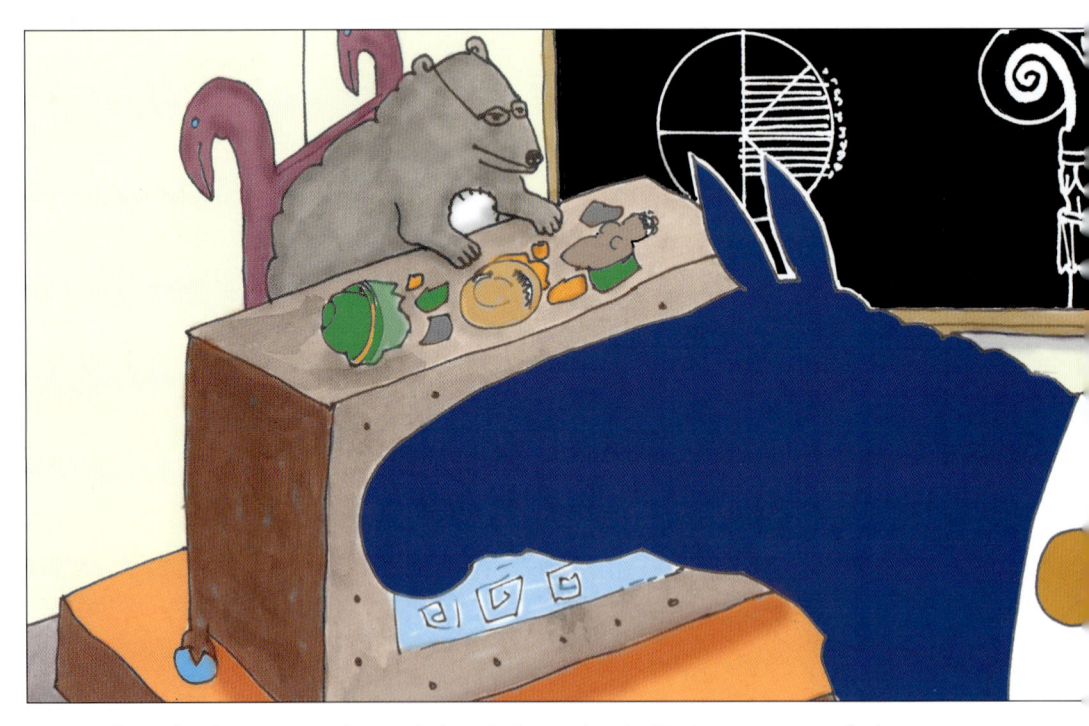

Soon though, the marmot's modulated drone leads Yeti to an extended nap, while Wombat assumes a meditative posture.

Indigo Animal begins to feel at home with these quiet animals, who exhibit none of the unchecked exuberance of the other LSRI students.

Indigo watches as Dame Eleanor arranges and rearranges the shards.

Imperceptibly, Dame Eleanor's mumblings become easier to understand.

"... now we see that many of the urns copied in later years and so popular at larger estates, have their antecedents in the funerary urns of the Etruscan civilization, this preservation by imitation being something to be thankful for, I suppose, but how sad then that there has been no similar interest in producing replicas of canopic jars. Please read Chapter One in your textbook. Class dismissed."

Wombat nudges Yeti and the
two depart together.

Indigo Animal remains behind, wanting to prolong these new feelings.
But now, questions begin to crowd in.

"Dame Marmot, why are there only three of us in your class? Why are most of the students more interested in those travesties of lawn sculpture I saw coming up the path to Orange Bearcat Hall?

Can a marmot be malevolent? It's difficult to know. But there it is—the narrowing of Dame Eleanor's eyes behind the thick glasses, and a momentary collapse of her tiny round ears.

Pulling a dusty copy of *Modern Trends in Lawn Statuary* out of the bottom drawer of her desk, Dame Eleanor turns it over to display the author photo on the back cover.

"This is why," whispers Dame Eleanor Marmot.

Later in the day, in Orange Bearcat Hall, bustling with students, Indigo reads that tomorrow morning there will be a tour, mandatory for all new students, led by the Director of LSRI, Orange Bearcat himself!

CHAPTER THREE
Tour of the Gardens

Next morning finds Indigo waiting with mixed feelings at the campus orientation. What could Dame Eleanor's enigmatic gesture have meant? But now a very large, orange and energetic figure strides towards them.

"Welcome new students!" Orange Bearcat begins boisterously, "You are *poised* at the **EDGE** of a world of LAWN ORNAMENTS that I could never have imagined when I was a young kit starting out!!"

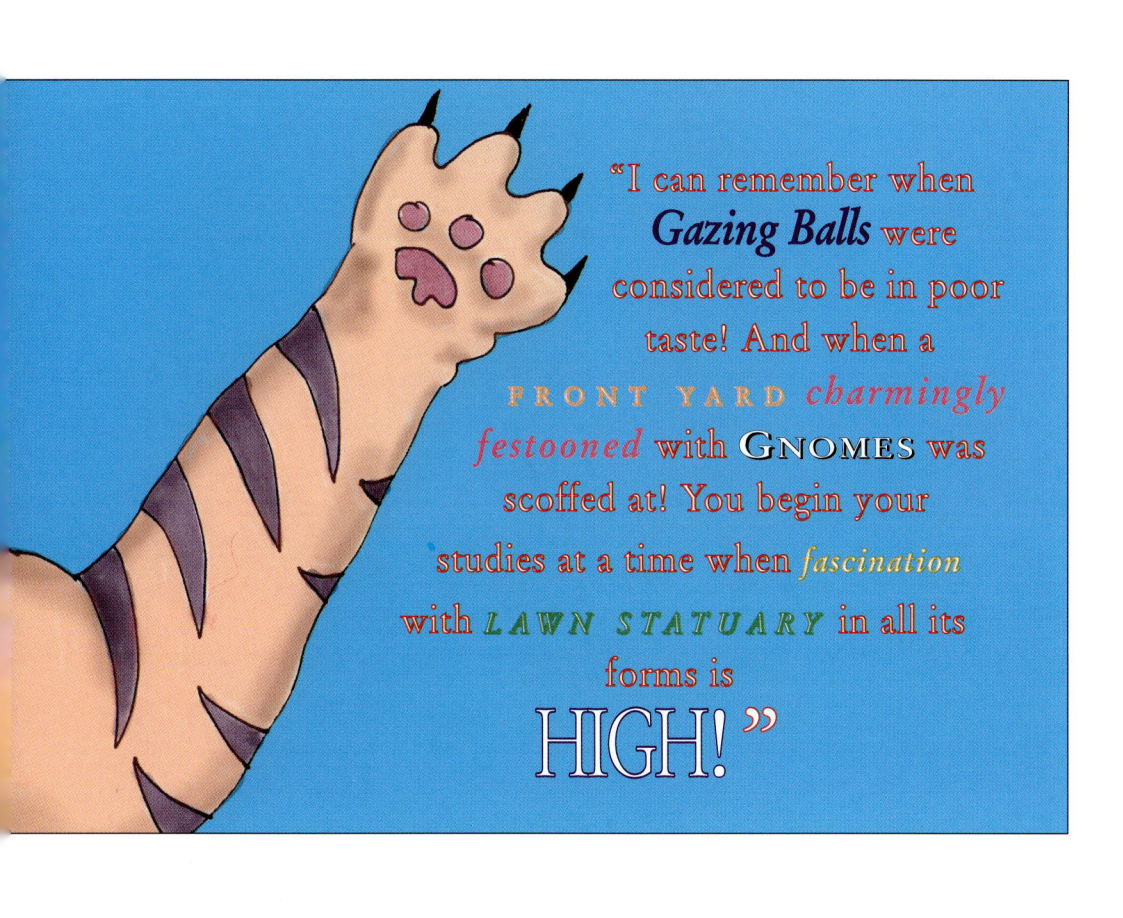

"I can remember when **Gazing Balls** were considered to be in poor taste! And when a FRONT YARD *charmingly festooned* with GNOMES was scoffed at! You begin your studies at a time when *fascination* with LAWN STATUARY in all its forms is HIGH!"

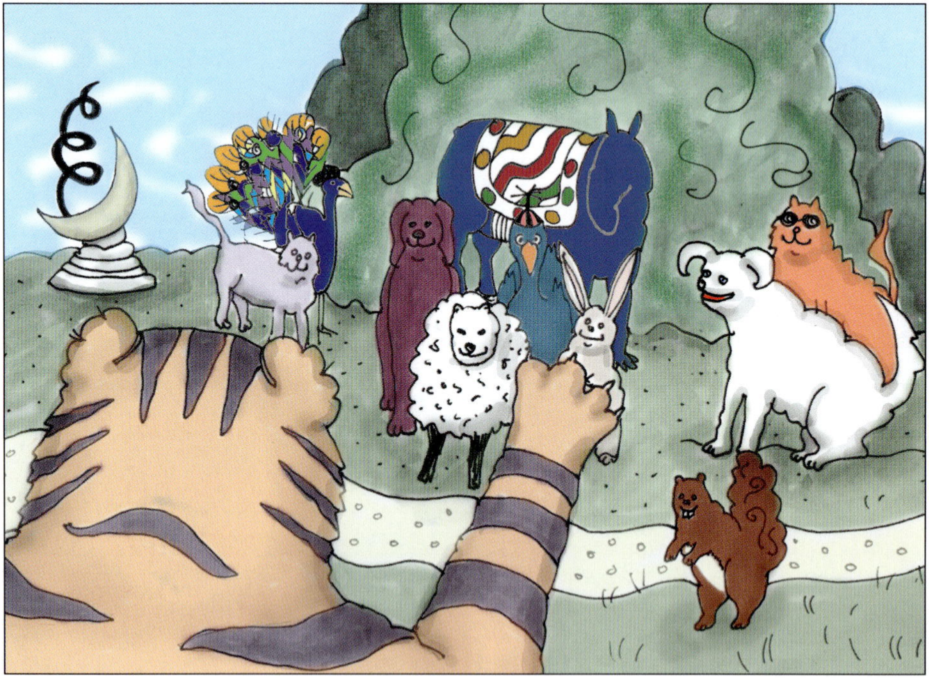

"After the great success of my book, *Modern Trends in Lawn Statuary*, I have made it my life's work to create here, at LSRI, delightful garden sanctuaries which present contemporary lawn ornament— in all of its infinite variety— according to a system of categories of my own devising!"

"Follow me now on a tour of examples of our most popular specializations.
There's so much to learn that we'll barely scratch the surface!!"

"What does any of this this have to do with *my* interests?" wonders Indigo.

Nevertheless, Indigo Animal finds some of the gardens inspiring:
the Japanese Garden

and the Egyptian Garden.

Indigo lingers in the Neolithic Garden and has to hurry to catch up to the group gathering in the Modern Garden.

Here Orange Bearcat's speech is peppered with unfamiliar terms—"Miro," "Braque," "Unified Field Theory," and "Cubist."

Entering the American Downhome Garden, Indigo Animal hears students squeal with delight.

True, a small clique of students affect an ironic stance toward the work.
Even so, Indigo Animal feels a sense of profound alienation.

The Postmodern Garden features a monumental topiary.

In the Product Placement Garden, Indigo Animal focuses on the ground and has to practice deep breathing and toe flexion.

Such attempts to relax continue as they enter the next garden, the very one that had been so dismaying on the first day of class. Orange Bearcat says,

"Yes, students! This is a collection of my own original work!"

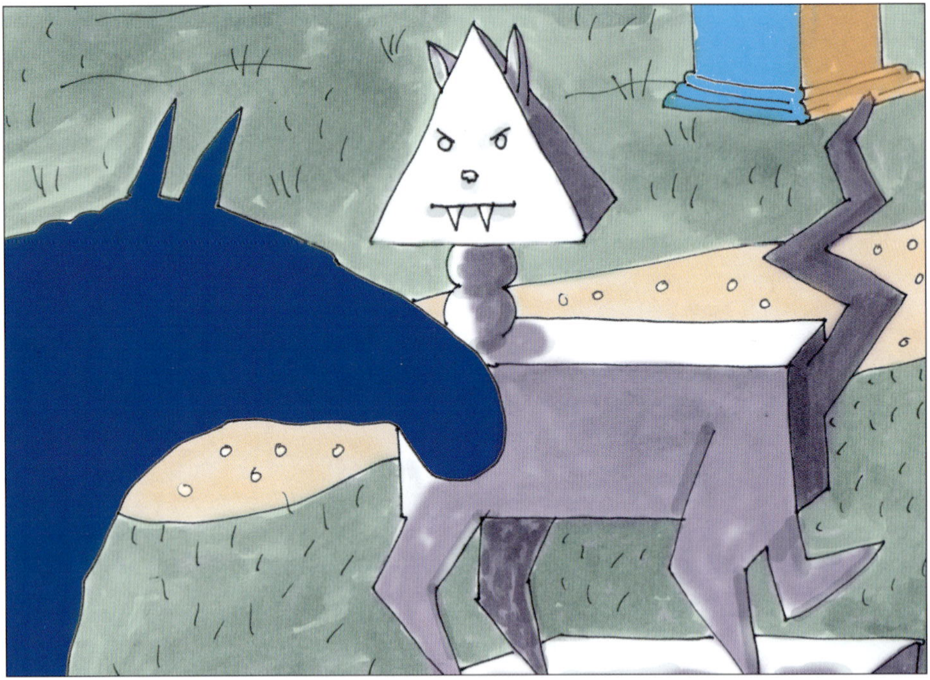

Looking around,
Indigo Animal wonders,
"How can the
Director of this Institute
let such bizarre anomalies see
the light of day?"

Preoccupied with grave doubts, Indigo trails along as the students crowd into the next garden, LSRI's collection of Country French Lawn Statuary.

"Aren't these splendid?" asks the Bearcat. "I know how much some of you are interested in the latest trends, so I've saved Country French for last!"

"Some might suppose a ribbon around the neck to be innovative, but WE know that this device is traditional—a constricted solution compared to the FUN we can have by opening up our minds just a little bit!"

As the students with tails begin thumping them excitedly on the ground, Indigo wonders, "Were these animals born yesterday?"

"Let me show you some truly creative themes that we generated last semester during the Country French Design Marathon. Who wouldn't be charmed by 'Pistolero Duck' here, designed by our own Neville Hare?"

Outwardly, Indigo Animal appears to be just another docile student, but inwardly, another process is taking place.

Thus Indigo Animal is confronted
with a moment of truth.
How otherwise to explain
the impulse arising from deep within,
which compels this otherwise
shy and retiring animal
to speak out?

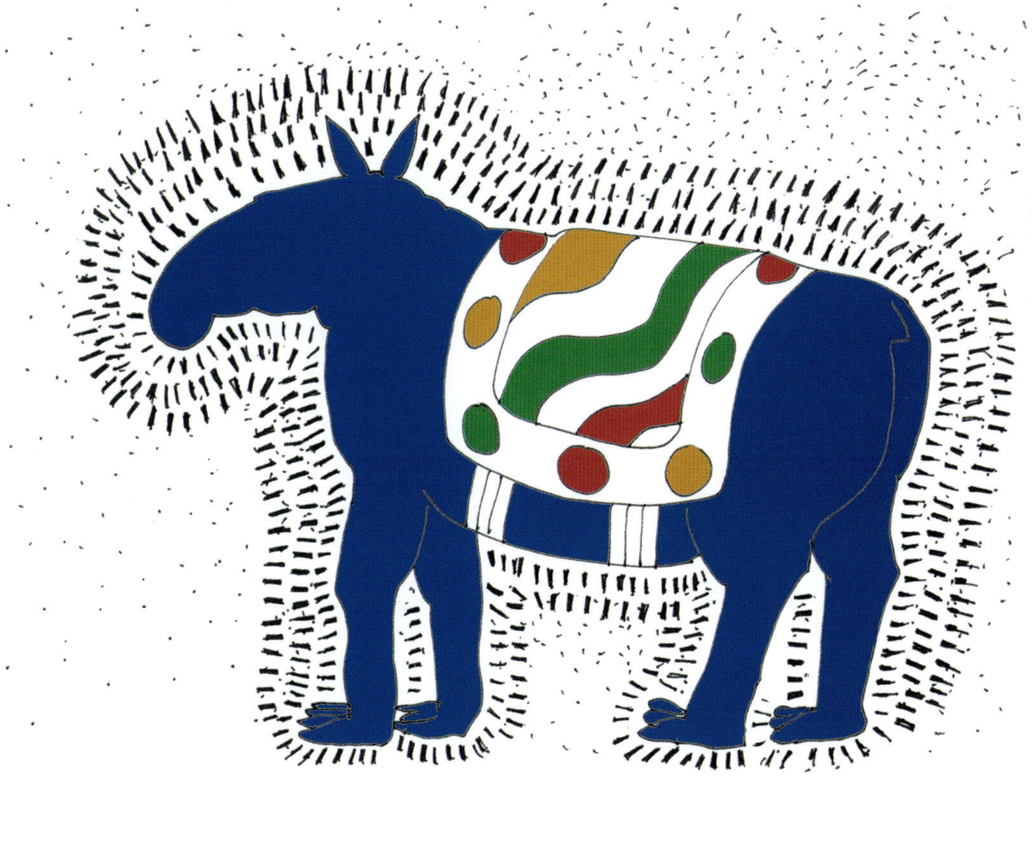

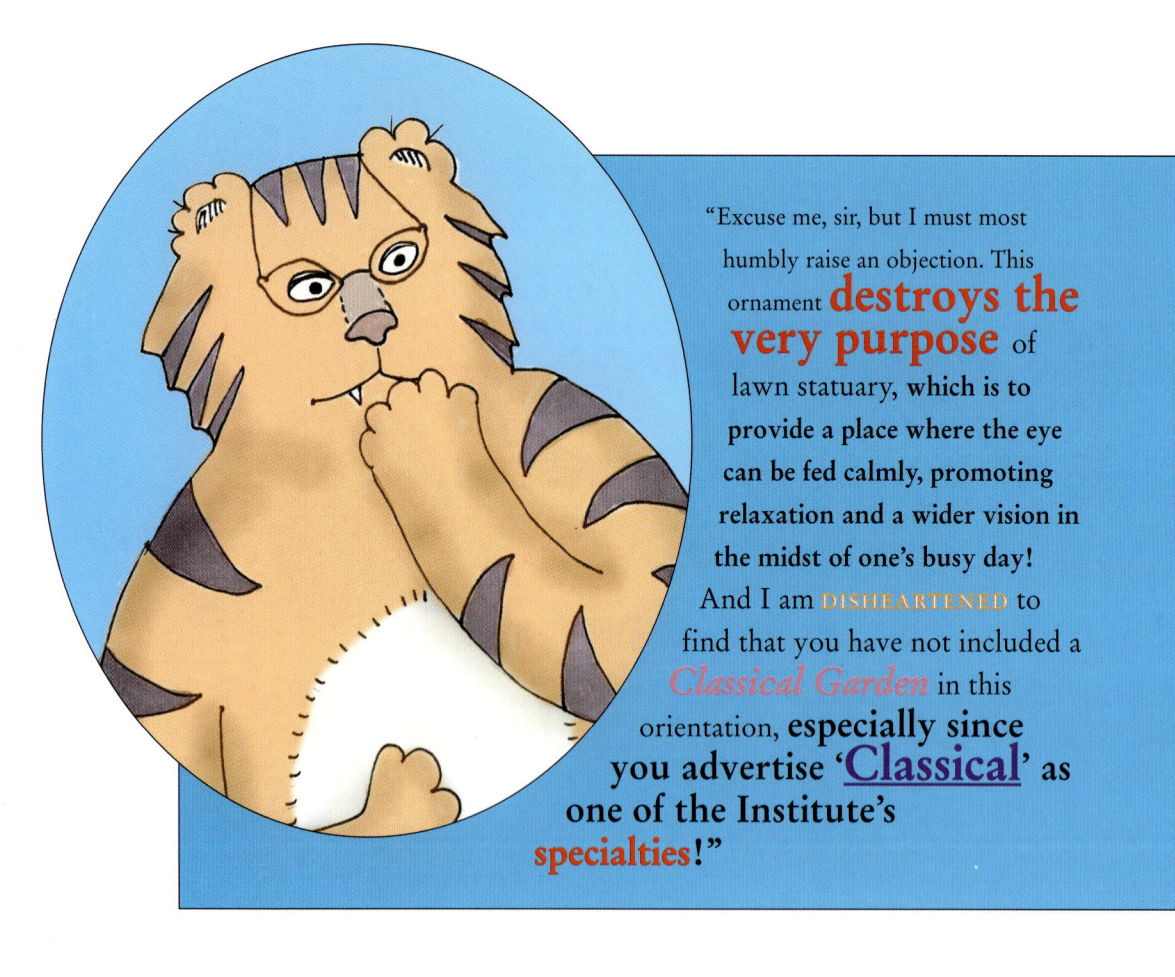

"Excuse me, sir, but I must most humbly raise an objection. This ornament **destroys the very purpose** of lawn statuary, which is to provide a place where the eye can be fed calmly, promoting relaxation and a wider vision in the midst of one's busy day! And I am DISHEARTENED to find that you have not included a *Classical Garden* in this orientation, **especially since you advertise 'Classical' as one of the Institute's specialties!**"

"Yesterday I attended an *excellent* class given by Dame Eleanor Marmot, and I will ask you what I asked her:

Why is there such low attendance in the Classical Lawn Statuary Studies Department?"

For a few moments, silence reigns. Then Orange Bearcat responds with the ease of an animal confident in his ability to prevail.

"I fear we have a traditionalist in our midst!" he whispers, and then solicitously, "What is your name?"

Indigo Animal replies, suddenly feeling vulnerable.

"My dear Indigo Animal," continues Orange Bearcat, "are you self-taught?" Indigo hesitantly nods yes.

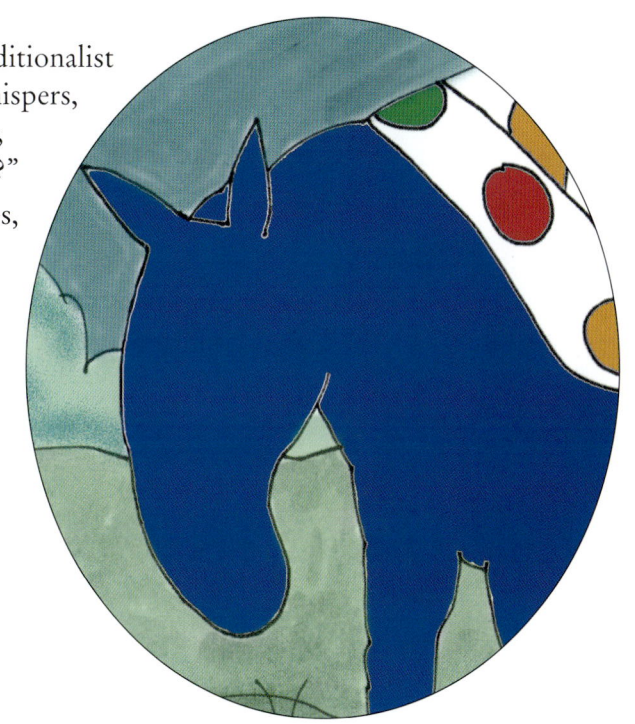

"Well, Indigo Animal, the old adage is true—a little knowledge can be a dangerous thing!"
Moving closer, Bearcat puts his arm around Indigo and continues:
"Indigo Animal, you're a smart animal! You've enrolled at LSRI! We're going to open up the whole UNIVERSE of lawn statuary to you!"

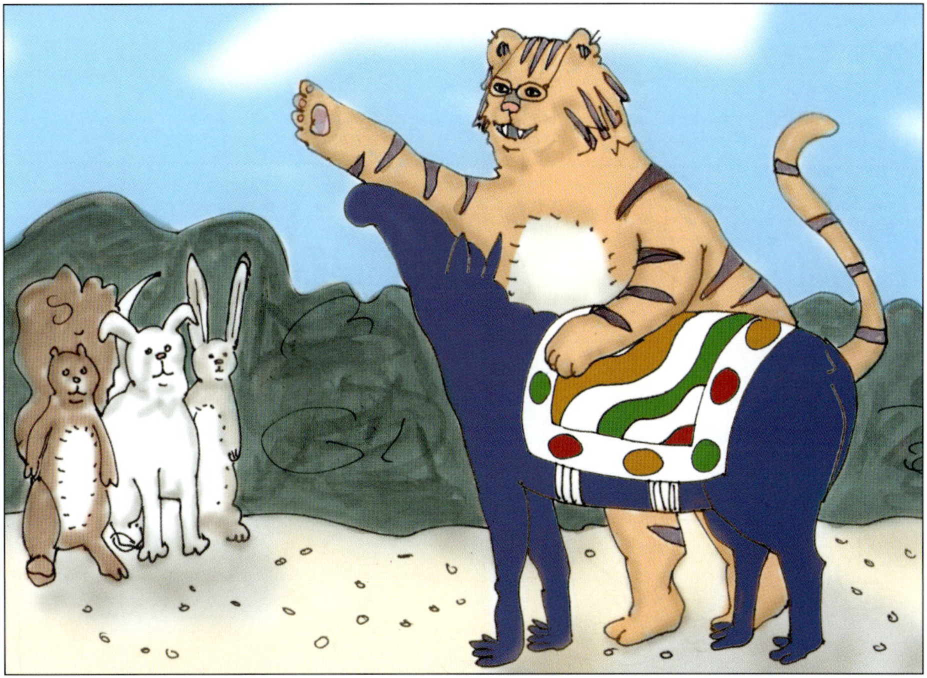

Bearcat continues, "Students, the question being asked is: 'Why are Classical Studies not more emphasized at LSRI?'"

"Well, let's visit the Classical Garden and find out!"

CHAPTER FOUR
In the Classical Garden

Indigo Animal, aware that this is the very path that the squirrel had pointed to on the first day of class, follows the group with renewed hope.

It takes awhile for the realization to dawn ...

... that this overgrown glade was once the Classical Garden so proudly described in the brochure.

Just then Orange Bearcat speaks. "Students, what do you think? We can't get anyone to look after the Classical Garden. Maybe it's just too boring."

Indigo might have been drawn into further confrontation by this insult had it not been for the effect of an inscription carved beneath a bust of Epictetus.

"*Think carefully before acting, for you will not be able to call back what has been said or done.*"*

*from Epictetus' *Fragments*

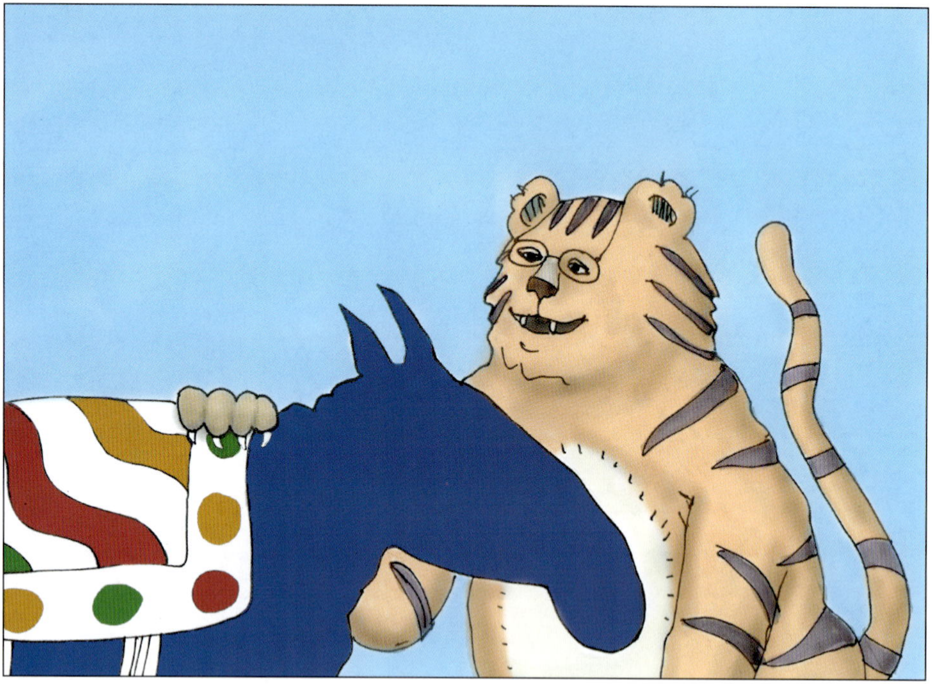

Indigo is still reflecting on this when Orange Bearcat says, "We have to face facts. Dame Eleanor, who I hold in high esteem, will be retiring soon; and when she does, the Classical Lawn Statuary Studies Department will be closed. Times change and we all must move on— even you, Indigo Animal."

Concluding, Orange Bearcat says to all,
"We live in a time when anything goes! Let's make the most of it!"

The students hurry to follow, but turning the corner, the Bearcat disappears.

Despondent, Indigo Animal remains behind in the neglected Classical Garden.

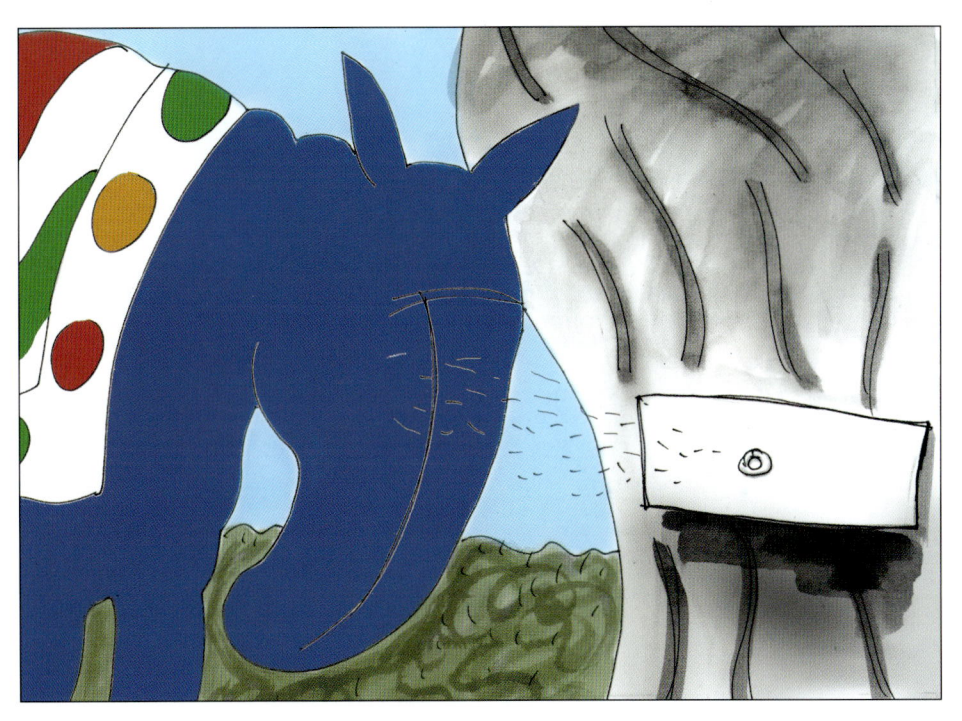

Eventually something at the back of a nearby sculpture,
just at eye level, catches Indigo's attention.

Is it a drawer?
Nudging it, Indigo
Animal discovers that it
opens, revealing
a hidden manuscript.

Sayings of my Favorite Ancient PHILOSOPHERS by Dame Eleanor Marmot

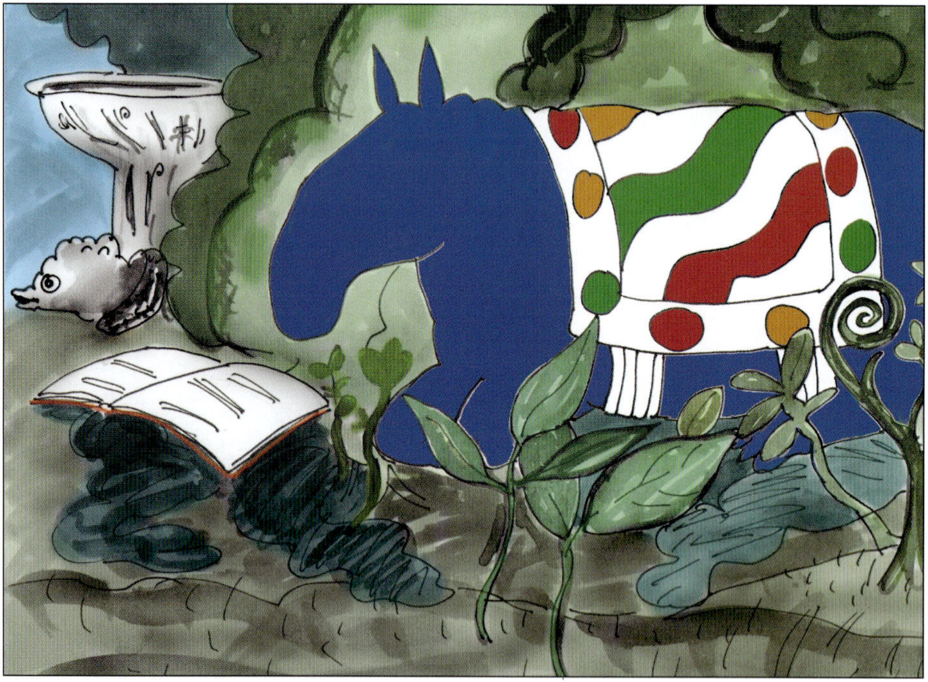

Nestling comfortably in a bed of soft weeds,
Indigo Animal opens the damp, slightly moldy manuscript
and begins to read. Dame Eleanor, it seems,
was fond of Marcus Aurelius:

"Look around you and you'll notice that all things take place by change. Get used to the idea that the nature of the universe loves nothing as much as to change the things that are and to make new things like them."*

*Meditations, Book IV.36

Later, walking home through the old neighborhood, Indigo Animal ponders another of Marcus Aurelius' statements:

"There is no evil in things which come into being out of change, just as there is no good from those things which are rooted in change."*

*Meditations, Book IV.42

Memories of Orange Bearcat's recent lecture continue to fuel Indigo's indignation. Struggling with inner turmoil, Indigo stops to consult the manuscript again:

"Are you angry with a man whose armpits stink? What good will this anger do you? With armpits like that, it is necessary that such emanations arise. 'But the man has a mind too,' you might reply, 'and he is certainly capable of realizing how offensive he is.'

Yes. And you have a mind, also, and can reason. Use your mind to awaken his.
If he listens, there will be no need of anger."*

"But why would Orange Bearcat ever listen to ME?" wonders Indigo.

*Meditations, Book V.23

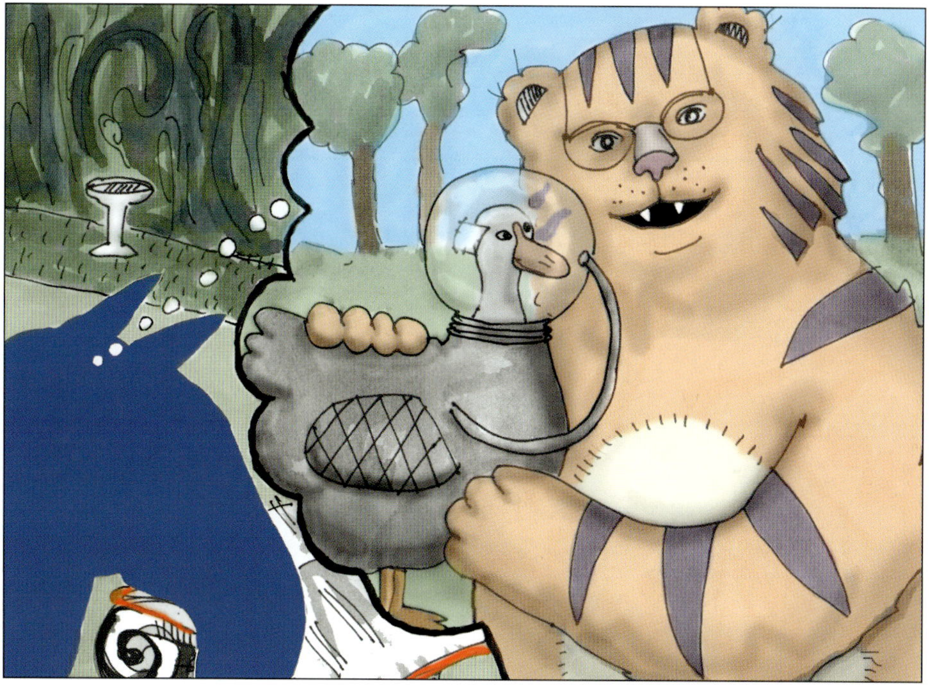

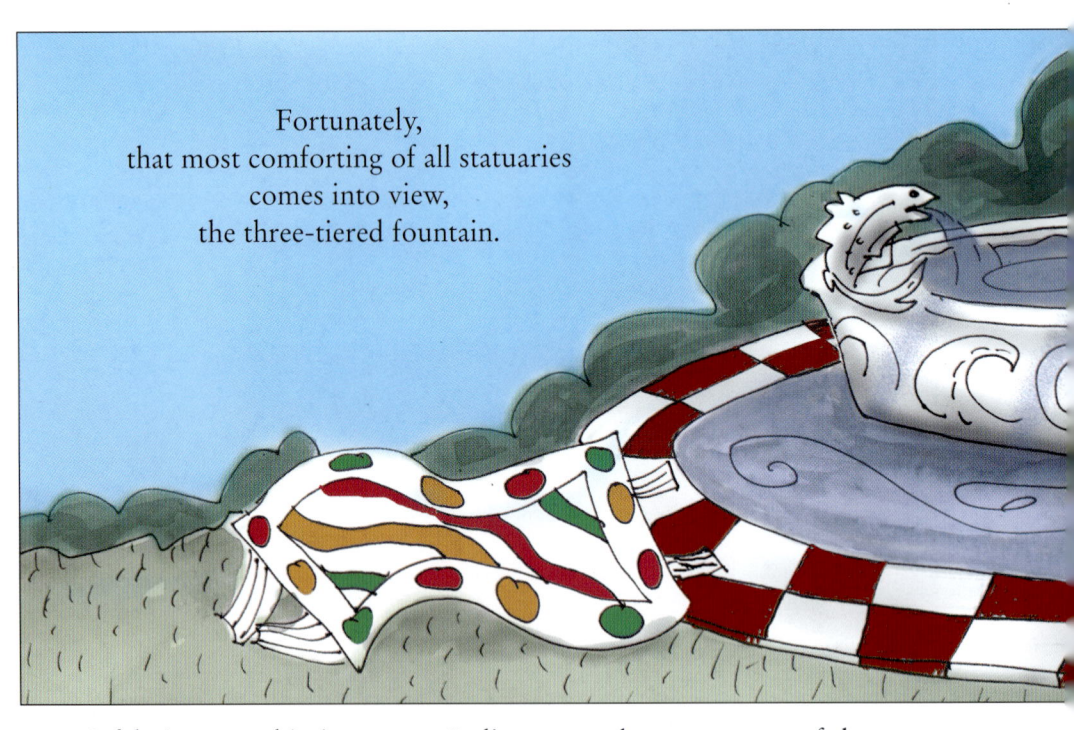

Fortunately,
that most comforting of all statuaries
comes into view,
the three-tiered fountain.

Safely immersed in its waters, Indigo remembers one more of the
thoughts which Dame Eleanor had collected: *"If something is difficult,*

don't conclude too quickly that it is impossible."* This thought, and the plashing of the fountain, eventually leads the way to a happier mood.

*Marcus Aurelius, *Meditations*, Book IV.19

CHAPTER FIVE
Recognition

Next morning, as Indigo Animal heads back to school,
the situation seems less in need of immediate resolution.

The ancient vessels assembled in the classroom restore that quiet state familiar to Indigo from study sessions at home.

This is fortunate because Dame Eleanor is deeply involved in her own research. When a timer goes off, Dame Eleanor, sighing, turns toward the class.

Once again tuning in to Dame Eleanor's mumblings,
Indigo enjoys the comfortable feeling of being in a safe place.

As the lecture continues, not wishing to sit in judgment of Yeti and Wombat, Indigo Animal merely appreciates their aptitude for slow, rhythmical breathing.

But at a certain point in the lecture,
Indigo Animal becomes uneasy, because
in the case of an exceptional krater, Dame
Eleanor is clearly misinformed.

"Excuse me, Dame Eleanor," whispers Indigo.
"This krater could *never* have been a birdbath!"

Dame Eleanor stops and stares at Indigo Animal.

Heartened by this moment of eye contact,
Indigo Animal ventures further:

"A French researcher, Jean-Paul Varan, argues that kraters represent 'a dialogue with the void.' From my own experience of bathing in … umm … fountains, I tend to feel a sense of safety and enclosure, the opposite of 'dialoguing with the void.' In my opinion, birds must feel the same thing while bathing in birdbaths. At least, they always seem to enjoy themselves quite a bit. So I've extrapolated from Varan's hypothesis and from my own experiences—and I cannot agree with you, Dame Eleanor. With all due respect, I must conclude that his krater could never have been a birdbath!"

Dame Eleanor does not reply immediately.

"Indigo Animal," she finally responds, "where Varan says 'the void,' others might say 'emptiness.' Do you think you *really* understand the meaning of these words?"

Oh joy! Indigo has never before experienced a scholarly exchange with a fellow lawn statuary researcher!

The Marmot suggests, "Indigo Animal, I think it would be a good idea if we had a meeting so I can assess your knowledge, the better to guide your studies." Thus begins a steady growth of trust and friendship between the two.

CHAPTER SIX
Treasure

One day, a few weeks later, while waiting quietly in the classroom for Dame Eleanor to arrive, Indigo hears a mysterious sound.

It seems to be coming from the broom closet. Looking inside, Indigo Animal sees a cavelike passageway. The sound calls Indigo to go further.

Soon enveloped by an impenetrable darkness, Indigo Animal feels disoriented. The ground beneath Indigo's toes is damp and slippery.

Still, Indigo continues following the sound.

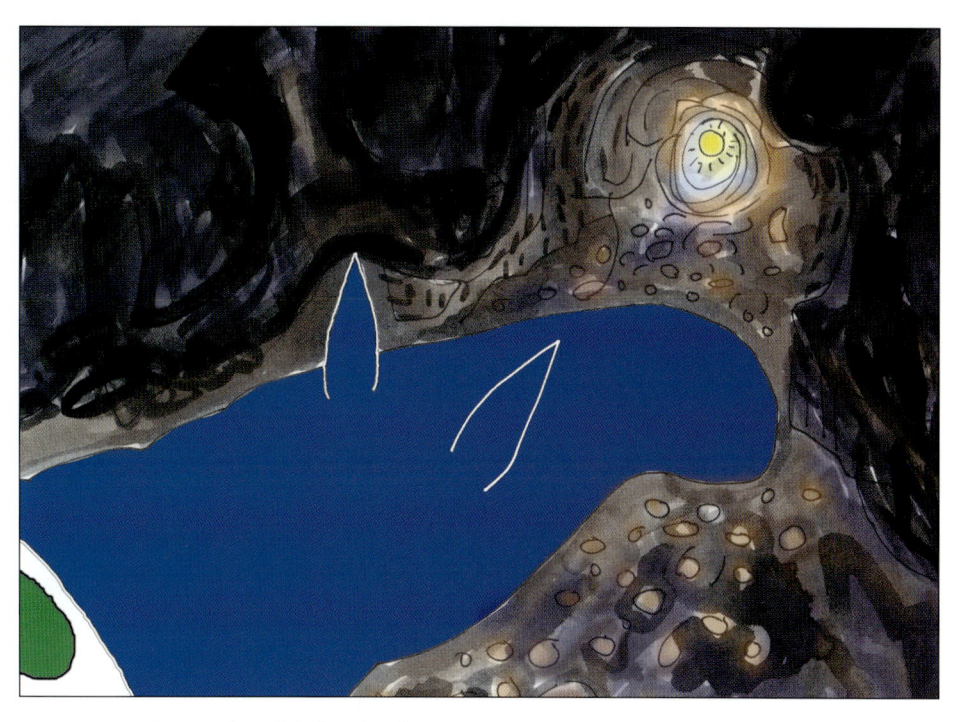

Just when it's beginning to seem too scary to continue,
the darkness gives way to dim light.

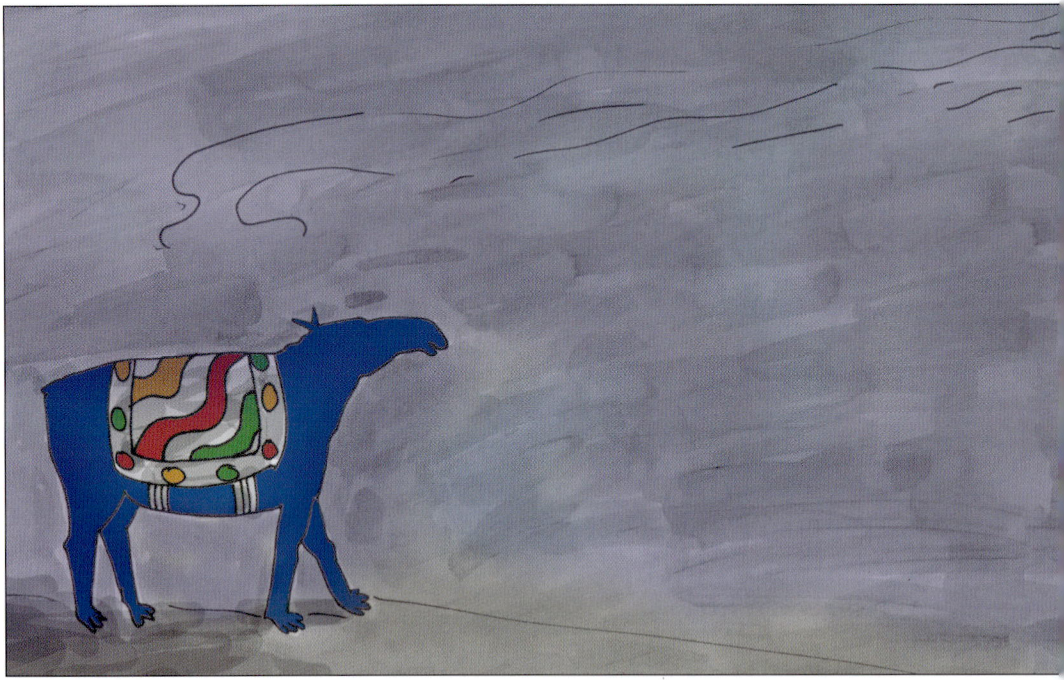

Finally, a figure comes into view. It's Dame Eleanor! She is singing!

"Indigo Animal, you have found me!" the Marmot exclaims.

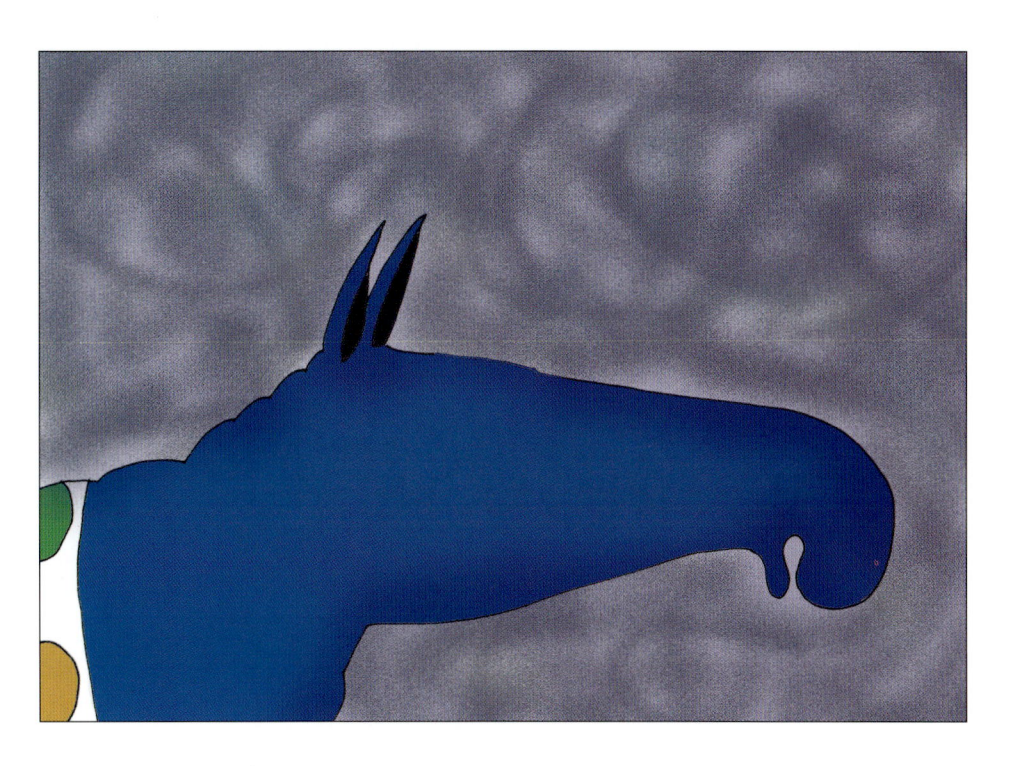

"Dame Eleanor, what were you singing?" Indigo Animal asks.
"I've never heard anything like it before!"

"It's an ancient ballad in the Aeolian mode. Orange Bearcat and I used to sing it together, but he has other interests now," says the Marmot with a sigh.

Then her mood changes as she says, "Indigo Animal, this is the first time that a student has ever ventured down here and found me!"

"You are a special animal, Indigo Animal."

Unaccustomed to such praise, Indigo examines the flutings
of an overturned column in the dim light.

Feeling encouraged, many questions now burst forth.
"Dame Eleanor, why are we here all alone in the dark?"

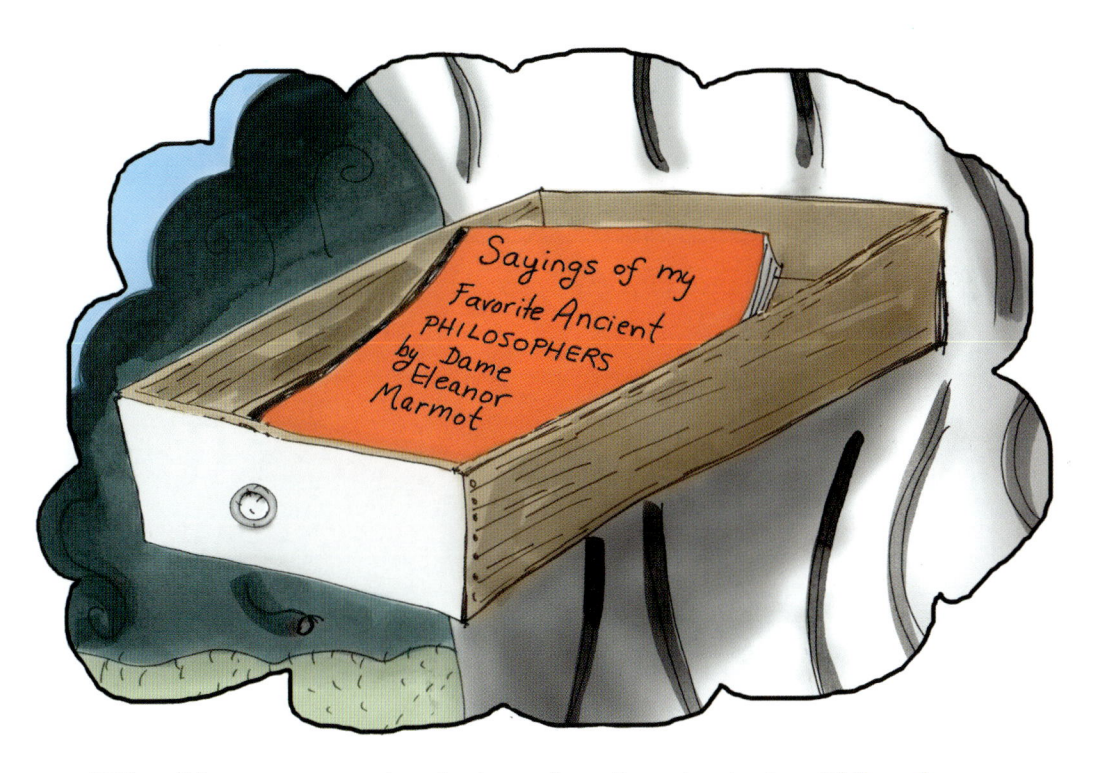

"Why did your manuscript, *Sayings of my Favorite Ancient Philosophers*, lie forgotten in a drawer?"

"And why is the Classical Garden so neglected?"

Dame Eleanor, moved that anyone cares, replies, "I will answer all your questions, Indigo. But first I want to show you some things that have been hidden away for a very long time!"

Dame Eleanor turns up the flame in the lamp, revealing a grand space, each corner piled high with statues, urns, sarcophagi, amphorae, columns, and fountains.

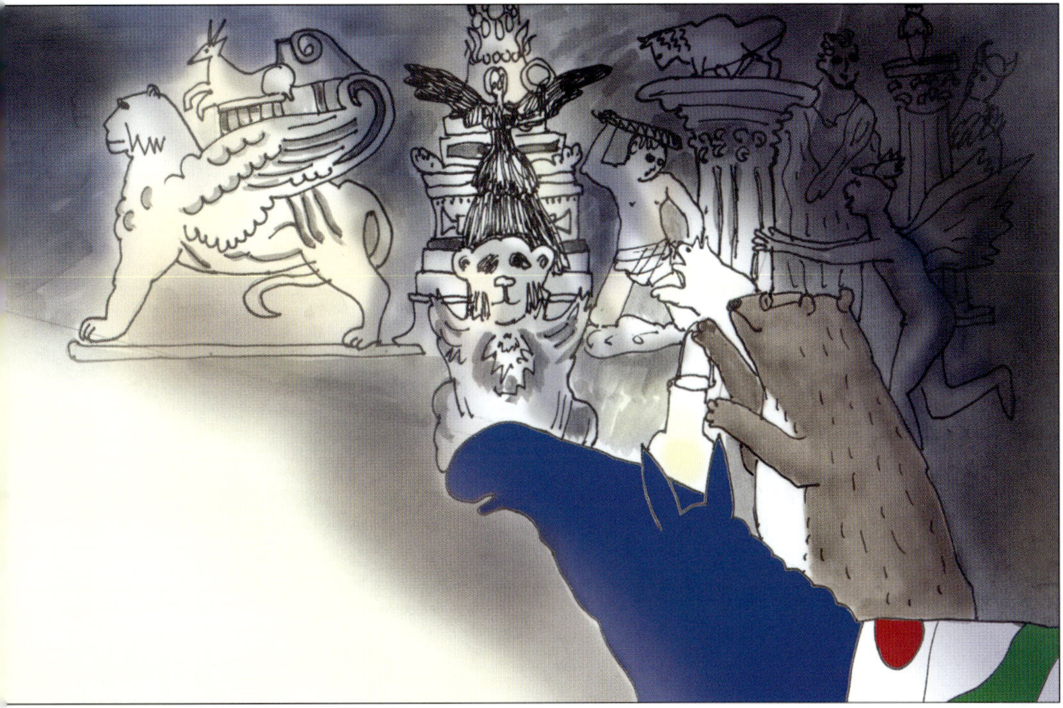

"But where …?" begins Indigo.

"There will be time for questions, Indigo Animal." Dame Eleanor replies soothingly "First, just try to see what's here."

"The statues I've seen are nothing compared to these!"
Indigo whispers with delight.

One piece in particular reveals the real quality of this collection.

Giving voice to a deep impulse, Indigo vows,
"This fountain must be allowed to gurgle once more!"

CHAPTER SEVEN
Ancient History

Dame Eleanor says, "I felt the same way many years ago when I first saw a photograph of this exquisite fountain."

"At that time I was Fountain Restorer to the Queen."

"Fountain Restorer to the Queen!" Indigo Animal exclaims. "Why wasn't this mentioned in the LSRI Brochure? That's a tremendous achievement!" After a pause, Indigo adds, "I didn't know you specialized in fountains."

"Oh, I did. I did." replies Dame Eleanor, suddenly more subdued. "It was all such a long time ago." Sighing, she looks at Indigo. "I suppose you're wondering why I left such an illustrious post to come here."

It's a complicated story. Suffice it to say that my tendency to isolate myself in the restoration room left me vulnerable to court intrigue."

"At the height of my difficulties I received a letter from one 'O. Bearcat'—
a request to come, all expenses paid, to restore this very fountain."

"When I arrived here, I found an extraordinary collection, in the possession of this enthusiastic but poorly educated young Bearcat."

"He so clearly needed my assistance,"
says Dame Eleanor, chuckling nostalgically.

"Orange Bearcat had something to do with this priceless array of artifacts?" Indigo gasps.

"Yes! Orange Bearcat collected all these beautiful specimens when he was barely out of kittenhood!" Dame Eleanor exclaims.

Seeing Indigo Animal's confused reaction to her revelation, she continues in a more soothing tone, "My dear Indigo Animal, Orange Bearcat's current dislike of classical lawn statuary can only be understood in relation to his past. Let me explain."

"Poor Bearcat! He might have grown up to be just an ordinary carnivore if not for a traumatic twist of fate."

"Stolen from his jungle home by poachers, he was smuggled across borders and then sold to an 'entrepreneur,' who soon tired of taking care of him."

"It wasn't long before the little Bearcat was being passed from one unloving owner to the next."

Dame Eleanor speaks in a surprisingly tender tone,
considering her usual reaction to Orange Bearcat:
"It's ironic, really. He himself was an exotic ornament."

"Having lost all sense of his natural identity, Orange Bearcat sought solace through the study of every fountain, amphora, and cherub that crossed his path. He often lived at big estates, you see, and that's what they had."

"Orange Bearcat was self-taught?! He asked me about that at the orientation. He acted like it was a weakness!"

"The Bearcat is full of contradictions," Dame Eleanor replies emphatically. "He's a driven creature."

"He must have been, to collect all this. How did he do it?"

"Under cover of darkness, Indigo—under cover of darkness," is all Dame Eleanor Marmot will say.

"I still don't understand why these *objets d'art* have been hidden in this cavern," Indigo Animal states.

Murmuring to herself, Dame Eleanor says, "I never took into account species difference with regard to energy level and performance output."

Then speaking to Indigo: "Orange Bearcat had more projects underway than I ever could have imagined!"

"He learned a lot on his own, but those gardens that you like—Japanese, Egyptian, and Neolithic—they exist through me! Of course we spent countless happy hours setting up the Classical Garden. It was magnificent."

"But I had *no idea* of all the work he was churning out after hours."

"Nor any idea of his research into genres which you and I would find beneath consideration. The success of his book, *Modern Trends,* was another factor in turning his interests, once so in tune with ours, into their exact opposite!"

"Orange Bearcat's new ventures were more commercially viable than classical research!" the Marmot barks, her narrative having stirred up turbulent emotions. "That's why all this statuary is down here!"

Then calling upon some inner resolve, she picks up a small relic saying, "In a way it couldn't have turned out more favorably for me!"

With my teaching schedule so greatly reduced, I have been able to devote myself to in-depth study of such worthy objects as this hammered bronze griffin head."

Indigo Animal imagines her working all alone in the basement, day after day.

"And now that you are here, we can undertake some *new* research!" Dame Eleanor concludes. Indigo Animal realizes that the moment has come when the truth must be told.

Taking a deep breath, Indigo says, "Dame Eleanor, at the orientation Orange Bearcat told us that you will soon be retiring. Then there will be no Classical Lawn Statuary Studies Department at all."

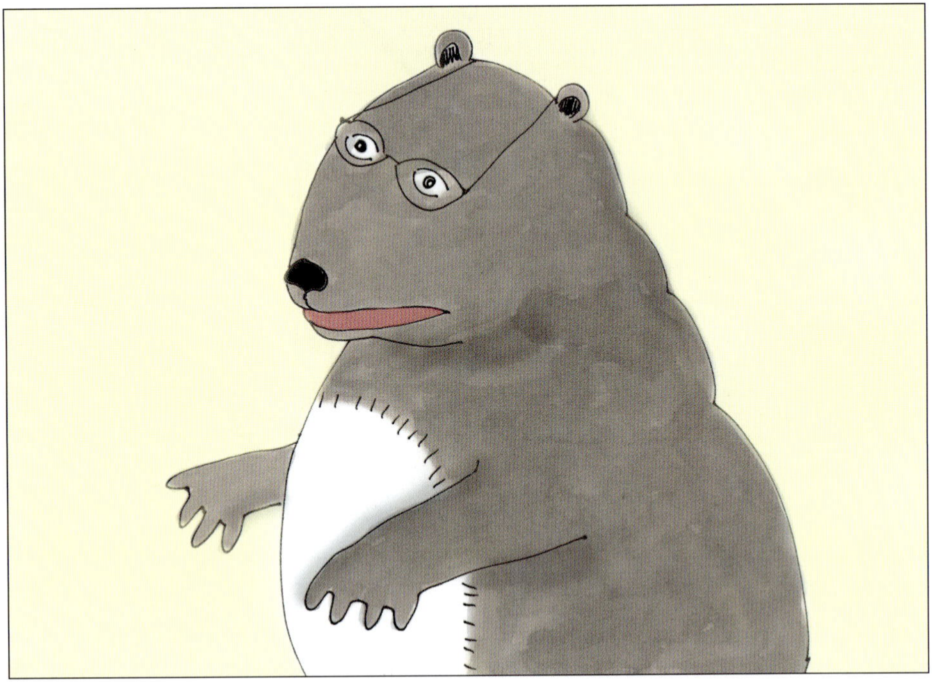

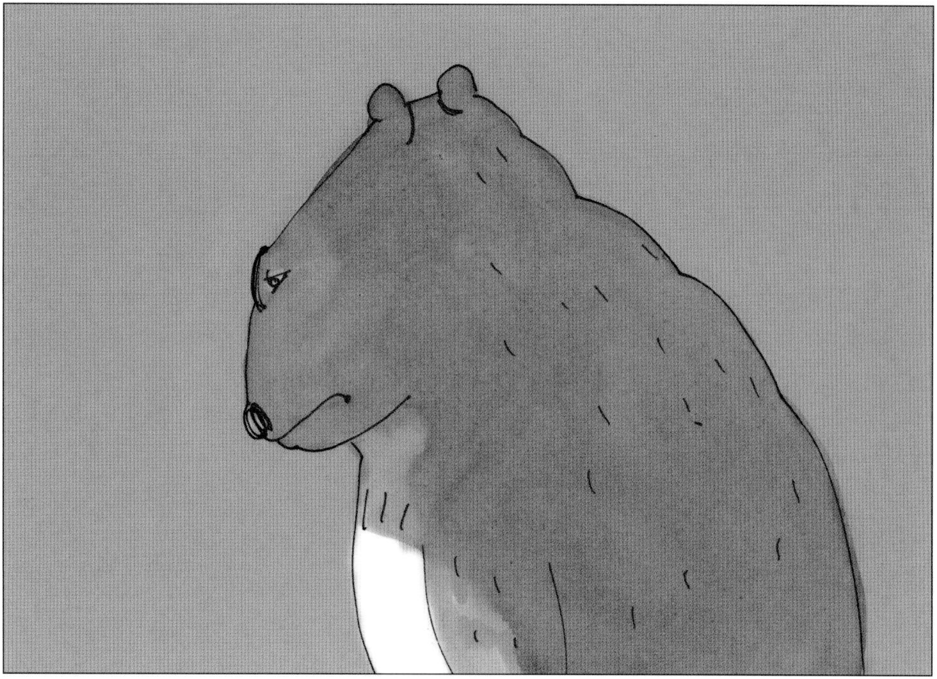

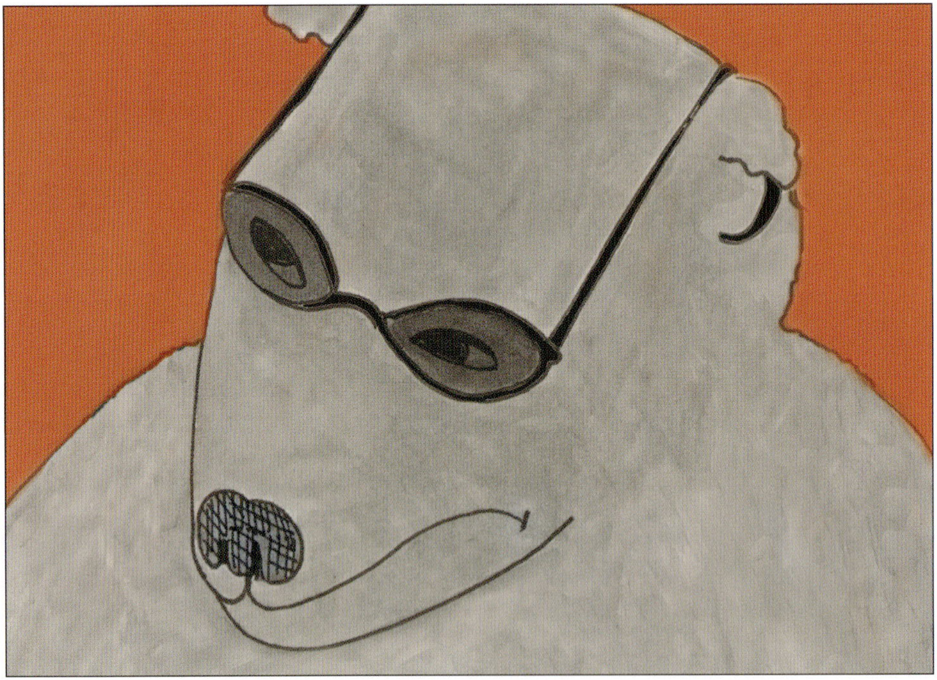

Ater a long silence, Dame Eleanor speaks, more to herself than to Indigo Animal.

"This changes everything! We will have to take action."

End of Book Two

Porch Lion Press Order Form

Name:_____

Address:_____

City:_____State:_____Zip:_____

I would like to order _____ copies of *Indigo Animal* at $9.95 per book.

I would like to order _____ copies of *Indigo Animal and the Lawn Statuary Research Institute* at $12.95 per book.

Make checks payable to: **Rue Harrison Whittaker**
Mail to: **P.O. Box 5008, Berkeley CA 94705**
Please add 8.25% sales tax for delivery in California.

Shipping:
Priority Mail: up to 3 books $3.85
Book rate: $1.50 for the first book and 50 cents for each additional book
(Surface shipping may take three to four weeks.)
First Class: $3.00 per book

For further details call *works + conversations* at 510.653.1146 or e-mail to publisher@IndigoAnimal.com. Write c/o Indigo Animal to Porch Lion Press, P.O. Box 5008, Berkeley CA 94705.

Visit Indigo Animal on the web at: http://www.IndigoAnimal.com